Breaking

A Poetry Book

Adam Levon Brown

ISBN: 978-81-19654-75-8

First Edition: 2024
Rs. 200/-

Cyberwit.net
HIG 45 Kaushambi Kunj, Kalindipuram
Allahabad - 211011 (U.P.) India
http://www.cyberwit.net
Tel: +(91) 9415091004
E-mail: info@cyberwit.net

Printed at Repro India Limited.

Contents

Your Whisper Changed Everything

Something jumped into my ear,
It was you,
talking me down
from the roof of my mouth
which wept only one word,

"Suicide"

Something collided into my ear,
It was you,

crashing the automobile
of my bumper-spinning mind,
which consumed itself in only one word,
"Death"

Something cried in my ear,
it was you,
the baby carriage
I once inhabited was gone,
and I am still here,
though it sits under the mobile spinning
only one word around in my eyes,

"End"

Something played music into my ear,

It was you,
holding the record player
of my eardrum close to your heart,
while I considered only one word,
"Escape"

Something rattled in my ear,
it was you,
holding the bottle
of pills I had planned to swallow
while ruminating on only one word,

"Deceased"

Something whispered into my ear,

It was you,

reminding me of all the best
times we had together;
all of the lunches,
how you taught me how to tie my shoes,
how you taught me to ride a bike,

how you always reminded me to put on my coat
before going outside,
worrying about me being cold,

Reminding
me of the days spent collapsing fears

with your words of guidance
and your ear of wisdom.

Your whisper changed that one word,
it changed it into danger signs
assembled en mass across every street corner of my mind,
while reciting only one word,

"Brother"

Your whisper changed that one word,
it changed
it into looking at skyscrapers from the ground up, turning
them into monuments of freedom,
while reciting only one word,

"Brother"

Your whisper changed that one
word,
it changed it into a yearning
to have a child of my own,
and a hope that this baby will never have to face
the mobile which once haunted
me, while reciting only one word,
"Brother"

Your whisper changed that one
word, it changed it into a symphony
played between us in open light,
while we laughed with no tears hidden

there to hold us down,
while reciting only one word,

"Brother"

Your whisper changed that one word,
it changed into a pharmacy, where medication
became the savior and not the enemy to loathe and distrust,
while reciting only one word,

"Brother"

I Knew I was gay
and I wanted to end my life

Your whisper-
Your whisper changed it all

First Time in a Psychiatric Unit

The line sits at the pseudo-God's feet, as he sits behind a reinforced window, ready to hand out medications

My insides begin breaking rapture with a primal scream
only I can hear

Fear is the casket which lies within

I sit idly, scratching the barcode strapped around my wrist

Breakfast, Lunch, Dinner,
the only 3 things to look forward to
when you're on hold in a psychiatric unit

Back to the line,

We stand as orderly as twin towers, waiting to swallow our next round of medication

I learned that the blue pills
give you the best high,
whereas the white pills make you itch

Medication is different for everyone, and I was learning the best mix for me

Fear is the casket which lies within

The alphabet on the calendar sitting on the wall seems to scream at me, yelling, "Get out of here when you can."

I look away from it, and continue pacing around the 30x30 common room

Another inpatient is rattling his head off about the government being after him.

He literally yells all day long, for hours about the same thing.

In any other setting, he'd be terrifying, he'd
be looked at as something less
In here, he was safe, in here, he had a name.

Fear is the casket which lies within

To the line again,

One of the patients I hadn't caught the name of suddenly punches the wall and demands that he talk to his lawyer. He then runs to his 10x10 room, equipped with a metal door and begins flipping over his mattress.
If there was a Jesus on this tiny secluded island of sterile floors and reinforced steel, it would be him

He then continues to berate the orderlies while kicking the wall next to my room

The orderlies act fast, and scream to one another,
"Grab the injectable, we need him settled down"

Lockdown means how it sounds.
It means you cannot leave

What they don't tell you is that you can't really stay either
It takes a certain amount of dissociation to be able
to live under the tight, freezing cold conditions

Fear is the casket which lies within

I guess that's why those who don't know,
and those who think they know, but don't really know
Look at us as C|r|a|z|y

Not because we're weak, or dangerous (Though some of us are)
But because they can see us deal with what they consider
insurmountable odds and rise from our inner caskets,
like a sort of Lazarus who eats and waits in line just to pass the time

Ragu

And so it goes,
and so it shall pass

My childhood was an open
bottle of Ragu, explaining
again and again, that
nothing was wrong.

The day my father
was questioned
for something
he never did

A spill of Ragu
tomato sauce
on a towel
I had used
to open it with

A hungry kid
with no food
in the house

Opening a can
of tomato sauce
to obtain sustenance

Mom had delusions
as she had struggled
with her disease

She was looking out
for me, and I praise her for it

The day my dad was questioned
for his involvement in what
my mother thought was rape

My agile mind at 10 quickly
knew what had happened

My mind was used to
combing through
tough situations
from an early age

My mind, my mind,
I thought I had lost it,
but it turns out
it was just Ragu

My mind, my heart
questioning my mother's
sanity at such an early age

My mind, my protectors
enraptured in battle

I knew what had happened
and I quickly told the police
that we had been
through this before

That my mom jumped
to conclusions
again and again

That my mom, bless her with all
of her protection, didn't know
that it was just Ragu
But what's done is done
and the past is an open
bottle of Ragu

My childhood is an open
bottle of Ragu, explaining
again and again, that
nothing was wrong.

And now, having been diagnosed
with anxiety and paranoia

My adulthood is an open bottle
of Ragu, explaining reality to myself

that nothing is wrong,
that nothing is wrong.

The Pool

The Pool,
my screams,
the shattered bone

Tears cascade
down my face
as I clutch my hand

The deluge
of your pained
strikes

My resistance,
the saltwater
strike to your raised
elbow

The Pool
My violence,
the gravity

of the chlorine
pushes against
my punches
to the solid
pool wall

The pool,
my screams,
my screams,

The ambulance
a rainstorm,
come to deliver me
The Siren,
The black-on-gray sprint,
the liquid rush

My cries,
the broken
abyss
The Pool,
the confusion,
the confusion

Metal Pins
placed surgically
into my hand,
hoping to hold
the crushed wave

The Pool,
my wrist,
my arm

Stranded swimmers,
singing for breath

The anesthesia,
Oceans

swallowing
my consciousness

The apologies,
drowned with hues of sadness.

The pool,
the forgiveness,
the forgiveness

The pool,
drained and vacant
for years to come

.

I Do not Sing the Body Electric

I shout it from the rooftops
30 years gone without a flash
and the big bang still says
he misses my fire
I tried to stand up, but God said
"Stand Aside"
I asked him if he meant stand behind,
because I'm done with that
I remember you saying,
"Don't stir the pot too much
or you won't have one to piss in"
I'm telling you now that the pissing contest has been over
since the moon decided to no longer call me its lover
Now I dance with the rain and Sun, rejoicing
in every lost tear I never shed for my own pain
Caught up in others' lives, no longer
speaking to my own in ways that resemble love
The rain decided to stay today,
where the Sun split like a soliloquy
from God's lips
I would have said goodbye to you
if my own tongue hadn't been the wind,
caught between two roofs hoping for deliverance
from a God I'll never truly know
I became the rain, loving clouds for their whispers
which held my tears in their bosoms for far too long
And now I can finally breathe
knowing that you feel
my pain, landing on you

daily like wet redemption
Brother, If you pray to the clouds,
you may receive either
a warm day or a hurricane
I'll be sure to tell you either way

Bullets

You told me you loved me,
though the words fell
from your lips like bullets
weighted with lead

Security threat, red.
Thoughts fired

If thinking could
free the mind
instead of enslaving it,
peace would be commonplace

Whenever I think of you,
I see the fires of my old home
and feel the grip of smoke
stinging my lungs like hungry hornets

Security threat, Orange.
Thoughts fired

If I could save you from those fires
I would, again and again

Though every time, in my dreams, I try
and fail to grasp you from my past

Sinking weights around the legs of my mind,
quicksand stains all that is me

Security threat, yellow.
Thoughts fired

When I finally do rest,
and I'm able to fully let you go,
know that you were my knife

Protecting my rib cage
from my stinging heart
while staining the stars
with drops of blood

Security threat, non-existent

I freed you one day
while walking with the Sun
on my shoulders

I spit you out like rays
slashing // the sky, hoping
for redemption from an angry God

I have bled all that I can for you,
as my wounds are nothing now
but memorial dust

I could sweep it all away
and keep you starving in saturated silence

Caught in orbit, the distance
between the Sun and Earth

But I'll keep you by my side instead,
tripping gravity with heels of granite

kicking the shins of every single meteorite
who decides to spurn you

Independence

I've counted and it takes
two cycles to disintegrate
my love for you

It has been four cycles today
and it's only Ten AM

The seconds slow and the
heartbeats begin

Where do birds fly when the nest is on fire?
Do they who stay behind
huddle for warmth, or simply burn along
with the memories of home?

The seconds slow and the
heartbeats begin

The memories, mouthed branches
with fanged twigs as full of lightning
as our past
Running from future lies
can only bring bruised bones,

sighing with shrills,
the fall from trust,
oh, the sweet, sweet blood

The seconds slow and the
heartbeats begin

Why do lies seek to bruise bones,
when already the truth eats
our hearts?
Where there were five seconds
to count the three syllables
of your name, there is now only one

The heartbeats stop and the
the naming begins

The last syllable is caught in my throat,
Tied to the last second, as I choke
on the ashes of my former home

Twelve Stanzas to Scream I'm Still Alive

You say that you love me
but you don't know
that I am a grave

When I say I'm a grave,
I mean my former
self before the Illness
is now gone

When I say gone,
I mean the darkness
reaches my eyes
even when I feel
on top of the Sun

Skeletons creep from my scars shaking
hands with pain
like it's a forgotten friend
I'll never admit I still see

Cobwebs infest my breath, gasping
for the spiders of the past to forgive my sins

When lies seek to hold
us inside the rib-cage
of our torment

Where do we
find the answers
for our hearts
to seek shelter in?

Do the lies collapse
upon the wounds
of our faith?

and when we truly are gone
body and dust,

will the hope
of being treated
the same as everyone
else linger?

Or become the reason
we hold hands in the end,

telling horror stories of how
we mistakenly thought
We never belonged?

Broken, the Motherless

The deception of my touch knows
no boundaries and yet fails to reach
the flawed rubied hearts of everyone I love,
especially you, my brother

I use the broken sonnets
in my voice to try to comfort you

I crush fears between my teeth when the silence sets in,
hoping to find the reasons why you chose
a dangerous life over us

I use the broken sonnets
in my voice to try to comfort you

I am misery incarnate, the quieted
muse in my veins cries for yet another
lonesome evening, while my heart
wants you here, fully sane again

I use the broken sonnets
in my voice to try to comfort you

The ashes we now share
cry for two sons caught
in a life filled with cruelty and turmoil

I use the broken sonnets
in my voice to try to comfort you

Fragmented lullabies of a forgotten family
hunger at my feet while the vision
of our once cherished life
crumbles before me

The sonnets then cry for us,
the motherless sons

The tourniquet sadness I use to salve
my wounds with has become ruptured

The sonnets then cry for us,
the motherless sons

If the voices in our song
could match the vibrato of my heart,
you would see how sorry I am

The sonnets then cry for us,
the motherless sons

The collapse of my faith has led
to our downfall, the blood of our sins,
leaving no survivors

The sonnets then cry for us,
the motherless sons

Our mother is dead,
and now there are no guarantees left
aside from my love for you

Voices from an Uncle Lost

You kept me as a kid
this entire time, drifting
through adulthood
with you on my mind

Your voice comforts me
in times of agony

You broke my anger,
lifted me in your arms
and sang me the holiest of sonnets

Your voice comforts me
in times of agony

I woke up today and found you
sitting on the newspaper,
your head draped in a halo
given to you by all of the people
you helped in your lifetime

Your voice comforts me
in times of agony

We didn't know
you were in so much pain,
that tomorrow would be the last,
that any time would be the final moment

Your voice comforts me
in times of agony

Yesterday you were here,
today you are gone,
and I don't know what tomorrow
will bring

Your voice comforts me
in times of agony

I just know that you won't
be here, and that alone
is reason enough to justify
carrying around this broken heart

Goodbye, my uncle
Goodbye, my heart

www.ingramcontent.com/pod-product-compliance
Lightning Source LLC
Chambersburg PA
CBHW022205160726
48282CB00024B/328
* 9 7 8 8 1 1 9 6 5 4 7 5 8 *